SIMPLE MACHINE PROJECTS

Making Machines with Screws

Chris Oxlade

heinemann
raintree

© 2015 Heinemann Raintree
an imprint of Capstone Global Library, LLC
Chicago, Illinois

To contact Capstone Global Library, please call 800-747-4992,
or visit our web site www.capstonepub.com

Edited by James Benefield and Erika Shores
Designed by Steve Mead
Original illustrations © Capstone Global Library 2015
Picture research by Jo Miller
Production by Victoria Fitzgerald
Originated by Capstone Global Library Ltd
Printed and bound in China by Leo Paper Group

18 17 16 15 14
10 9 8 7 6 5 4 3 2 1

Library of Congress Cataloging-in-Publication Data
Oxlade, Chris, author.
  Making machines with screws / Chris Oxlade.
     pages cm.—(Simple machine projects).
  Includes bibliographical references and index.
  ISBN 978-1-4109-6802-9 (hb)—ISBN 978-1-4109-6809-8
(pb)—ISBN 978-1-4109-6823-4 (ebooks) 1. Screws—Juvenile
literature. 2. Simple machines—Juvenile literature. I. Title.

  TJ1338.O88 2015
  621.8'11—dc23   2014013822

**This book has been officially leveled by using the F&P Text
Level Gradient™ Leveling System.**

Acknowledgments
We would like to thank the following for permission to
reproduce photographs: All photos Capstone Studio: Karon
Dubke except: Alamy: David Gee 4, 21; BigStockPhoto.com:
dragon_fang, 29 (bottom); Dreamstime: Richard Lister, 7;
Shutterstock: Boris Bulychev, 4, Diana Taliun, 20, Digoarpi, 9,
Isantilli, 29 (top), Julija Sapic, 14, Kondrashov Mikhail Evgenev-
ich, 15, Madlen, 26, RMIKKA, 8, wavebreakmedia, 27.

Design Elements: Shutterstock: Timo Kohlbacher.

We would like to thank Harold Pratt and Richard Taylor for
their invaluable help in the preparation of this book.

CONTENTS

Some words are shown in bold, **like this**. You can find out what they mean by looking in the glossary.

WHAT ARE SCREWS?

You have probably joined together the pieces of a model kit with **nuts** and **bolts**, or attached a battery cover with a small screw. And you must have put the lid on a bottle. Then screws have helped you.

When scientists use the word "screw," they mean a screw thread, like the thread on a bolt or on a **fastening screw**. In this book, examples of screws and practical projects will help you to understand how screws work.

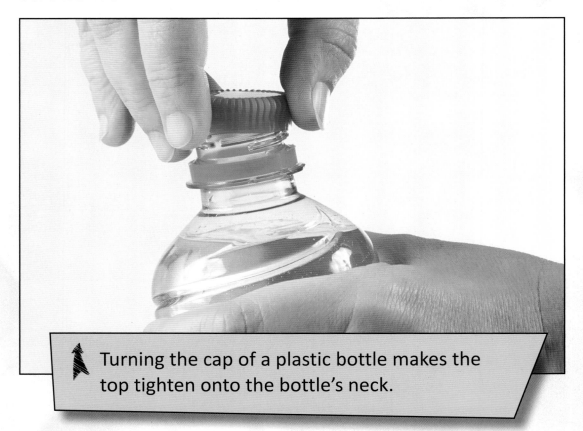

Turning the cap of a plastic bottle makes the top tighten onto the bottle's neck.

Screws around us

Almost every machine and device, from toy cars to giant airliners, has screws that join its parts together. The chairs, beds, and tables in your home are also held together by screws.

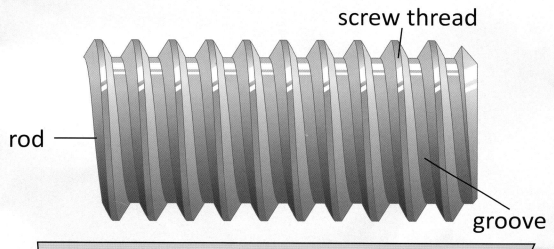

screw thread

rod

groove

 A screw is a rod with a spiral thread around it.

SIMPLE MACHINES

Simple machines help us to do jobs such as lifting loads and gripping objects tightly. Screws are one of the five types of simple machines. The others are the **lever**, the **pulley**, the **wheel and axle**, and the **ramp** and **wedge**. Also, **springs** are like simple machines.

HOW SCREWS WORK

Remember that when we use the word "screw," we mean a screw thread. Imagine a screw with its thread interlocking with a material. An example of this would be a fastening screw in a piece of wood. When you turn the screw with a screwdriver, the screw pushes or pulls on the material.

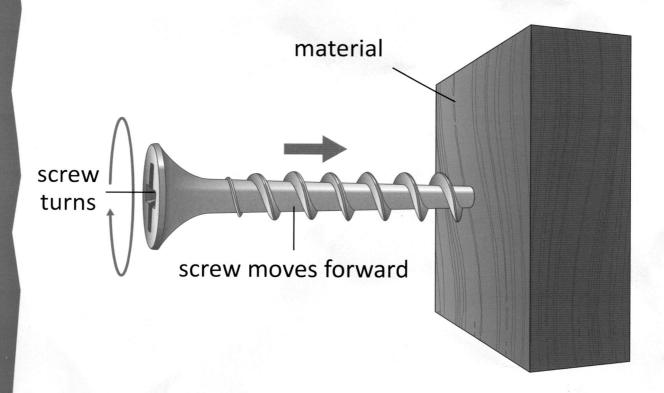

material

screw
turns

screw moves forward

 This diagram shows that when you turn a fastening screw **clockwise**, it moves forward

When turning a fastening screw with a screwdriver, a screw forces itself into wood.

Increasing force

The force a screw makes on a material is greater than the force you use to turn the screw. It is the screw thread that increases the force. That's how a screw can force its way into a hard piece of wood.

FORCE AND MOTION

Simple machines such as screws can change force and motion (movement). A simple machine can make a force (a push or a pull) larger or smaller, or change its direction. It can also make a movement larger or smaller, or change its direction.

USING SCREWS

The most common job of a screw is to attach things together. A screw thread can hold an object onto a piece of material, or it can pull two pieces of material against one another.

Screws for gripping

A fastening screw has a sharp end and a wide head. There is a slot in the head that a screwdriver fits into. When you turn a fastening screw, the thread grips the material the screw is in (such as wood or plastic) and pulls itself into the material.

slots for screwdriver

screw thread

This is a fastening screw for wood.

Nuts and bolts

When you turn a nut that is on a bolt, the nut moves along the bolt. Any materials that are squeezed between the nut and the head of the bolt are then held tightly.

bolt

nut

Pieces of metal are joined together with nuts and bolts.

CLOCKWISE AND COUNTERCLOCKWISE

Most screws have clockwise threads. This means when you turn the screw clockwise, the screw thread moves the screw away from you. When you turn the screw **counterclockwise**, the screw thread moves it toward you.

Screw Threads

This project will help you to understand how the screw threads on screws work.

WARNING!
Ask an adult for help using sharp objects.

What you need:
- some scraps of softwood (such as pine)
- a hammer and small nail
- some small wood screws, about 1 in. (3 cm) long
- a screwdriver that fits the slots in the screws

1 Take one scrap of wood. Gently hammer a nail into the center of the wood to make a small hole.

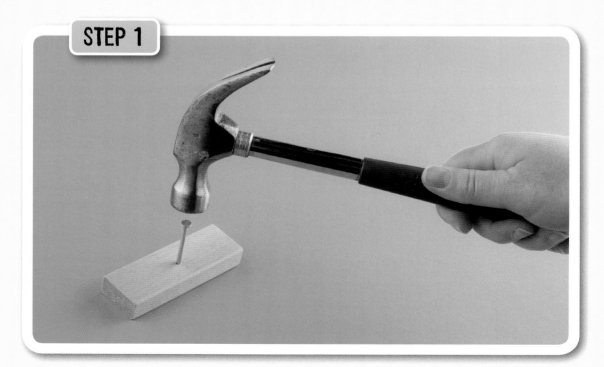

STEP 1

2 Push the sharp end of a screw into the hole you have made in the wood.

3 Insert a screwdriver into the head of the screw and turn slowly clockwise (see picture). You may need to hold the wood and perhaps the screw to begin with.

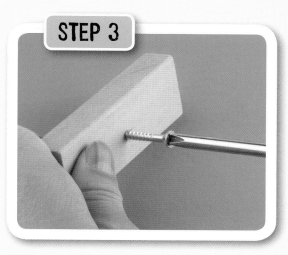

STEP 3

4 Keep turning the screw until about two-thirds of its thread is in the wood.

5 Now turn the screwdriver counterclockwise to see what happens to the screw.

What did you find out?

When you turn a screw, the thread of the screw pulls the screw into the wood. The thread grips the wood very tightly, so you can't pull the screw out.

Working with Nuts and Bolts

Try this project to see how the screw thread on a nut and bolt work together.

1 Put one nut on the bolt and turn it clockwise until the nut is about halfway along the bolt.

2 Hold the nut and turn the bolt clockwise. Then turn the bolt counterclockwise to see how the bolt moves through the nut.

STEP 2

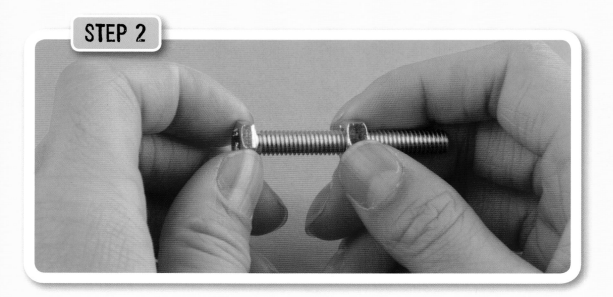

3 Cut two pieces of corrugated cardboard 4 x 4 in. (10 x 10 cm). With a sharp pencil, pierce a hole in the center of each piece of cardboard.

STEP 4

4 Push the bolt through both pieces of cardboard until the cardboard rests against the nut (see picture). Now put the other nut on the bolt.

STEP 5

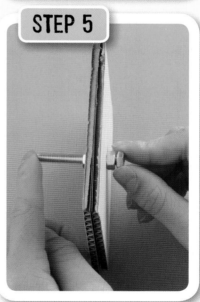

5 Turn the second nut clockwise until it touches the cardboard. Now turn both nuts with your fingers. Find the best way to turn the nuts in order to make the pieces of cardboard squeeze together.

What did you find out?

The screw thread on the bolt grips the screw thread on the inside of the nut. Turning both nuts gently with your fingers can squeeze the pieces of cardboard together tightly.

LIFTING AND GRIPPING WITH SCREWS

We sometimes use screws to lift or grip objects. Because screws can make forces larger, you can lift heavy things or grip things tightly by making a small push or pull.

Scissor jack

A scissor jack (also called a screw jack) is a machine that uses a screw thread to lift a car. This makes changing a car wheel easier. Turning the jack's handle turns a screw thread. This pulls the two sides of the jack together, and this pushes the car upward.

handle

This jack lets a driver lift a heavy car with a gentle turn of its handle.

Vises

A vise is a tool that holds a piece of material while you cut or shape it with tools such as saws and files. You move together the two jaws of the vise by turning a screw thread.

jaws

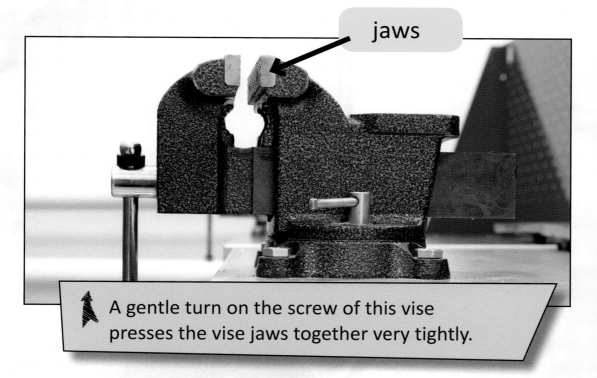

A gentle turn on the screw of this vise presses the vise jaws together very tightly.

PRINTING

For hundreds of years, printing presses had huge wooden screw threads. The screw thread pressed blank sheets of paper firmly onto metal letters covered with ink. This transferred the ink to the paper.

Making a Jack

In this project, you can make a model jack. Use the jack to lift a small plank of wood with just one finger!

What you need:
- some thick cardboard
- a sharp pencil
- a bolt about 4 to 6 inches (10 to 15 cm) long
- 2 nuts to fit the bolt
- a washer to fit the bolt
- 2 popsicle sticks
- 2 medium rubber bands
- the cap from an old felt-tip pen
- a small plank of wood
- a heavy book

1 Cut a square of cardboard 4 x 4 in. (10 x 10 cm). Pierce a hole in the center of the cardboard with a sharp pencil (see picture). The hole should be smaller than the width of your selected bolt.

STEP 1

2 Push the bolt through the hole so the bolt head is against the cardboard.

3 Screw a nut onto the bolt until it is tight against the cardboard. You might need to bend the cardboard to make a stable base.

4 Put two popsicle sticks together face to face. Wrap a rubber band around the sticks about 1 in. (2 cm) from one of the ends (see picture below).

STEP 4

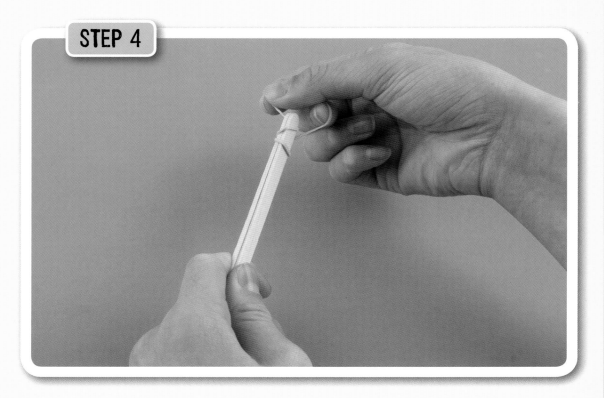

5 Trap the second nut between the two sticks. Push the ends of the sticks together and put a rubber band around these, too. You might need somebody to help you by holding the sticks together.

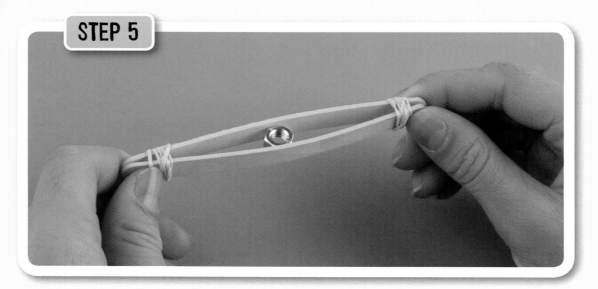

STEP 5

6 Place the trapped nut on the end of the bolt and wind the sticks around and around until the nut is about halfway down the bolt.

7 Put a washer onto the bolt. Then put the pen cap over the washer (see picture, right).

STEP 7

8 Balance the small plank of wood with one end on a heavy book and the other end on the jack (as in the picture for step 9).

9 Now carefully wind the popsicle-stick handle counterclockwise to lift the wood (as shown below).

STEP 9

What did you find out?

Try lifting the end of the wood with one finger to see how much force you need. Compare that push to the push you needed on the popsicle-stick handle to raise the wood. The jack made the effect of your small push much larger.

MOVING MATERIALS WITH SCREWS

Screws can also move loose materials, such as powder and beads. A screw thread with a deep groove traps materials between the thread. When the screw turns, the materials are pushed or pulled along the thread.

A soil auger is a screw that moves soil. Construction workers use augers to drill deep holes in soft ground. Drill bits have screw threads that move material out of the hole that is being drilled.

The auger's screw thread lifts the soil from a hole.

SHIP SCREWS
The propellers of ships are sometimes called screws. That's because they work like screw threads, pushing water backward to move a ship forward.

Moving liquids

Screws can move liquids, too. A machine called an Archimedean (say "arc-ee-meed-ee-uhn") screw lifts water. It is made up of a screw thread inside a tight-fitting tube. As the screw is turned, the water moves upward, trapped between the threads.

Archimedean screws are still used in some parts of the world to raise water from rivers onto fields.

Make an Archimedean Screw

In this project, you can see how a screw thread moves materials when it turns, just like an Archimedean screw.

1 Place the disc (such as a can) on a piece of cardboard and draw around it. Stand the tube in the center of this circle and draw around it.

What you need:
- some cardboard
- a disc about 1 in. (2 cm) wider than your tube (such as the base of a can)
- a cardboard tube, such as a cut-back paper towel tube (ask an adult to cut this)
- scissors
- sticky tape
- a large (2 liter) plastic bottle
- some marbles

STEP 1

2 Cut out the larger circle. Now cut in from the edge of this disc to the inner circle, and then around the inner circle. You should end up with a ring of cardboard with one cut in it (see picture, right).

STEP 2

3 Put the ring around your tube. Tape one end of the ring to the end of the tube. Tape the other end of the ring to the tube, about 1 in. (2 cm) along the tube from the end.

4 Use a couple of small pieces of sticky tape to attach the ring to the tube. This means the ring stays in the shape of a screw thread.

STEP 4

5 Make another ring in the same way. Fix one end of the ring to the end of the first ring. Fix the other end to the tube, about 1 inch farther along the tube.

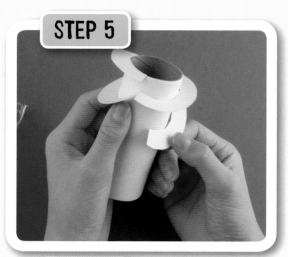

STEP 5

6 Add another two rings in the same way to complete the screw thread (see picture, right).

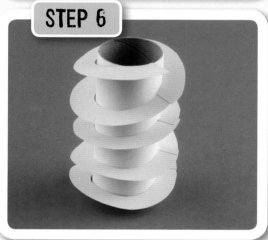

STEP 6

7 Ask an adult to help you here. Cut the top and bottom off the plastic bottle to leave a tube with parallel straight lines about 6 in. (15 cm) long.

8 Cut a straight line along the plastic tube (see below).

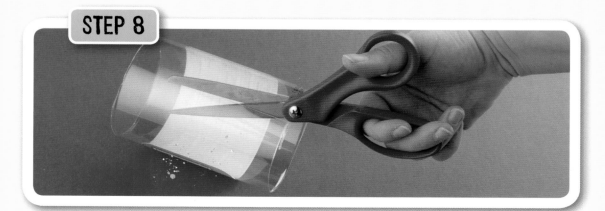

STEP 8

9 Fold the plastic gently around the screw thread. The tube should touch the thread, but not squeeze it. Stick the edges of the tube together.

10 Put the tube on your work surface. Put some marbles in one end of the tube (see picture below).

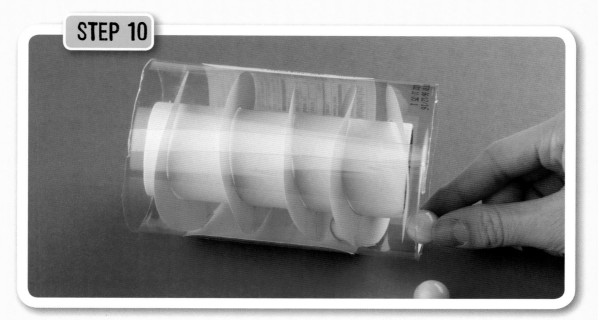

STEP 10

11 Keep the bottle still. Turn the screw clockwise or counterclockwise. The screw thread collects the marbles and moves them along the tube.

What did you find out?

The screw thread moves the marbles because the marbles become trapped in the thread of the screw. Try turning the screw thread the other way, too.

SCREWS IN COMPLEX MACHINES

Many complicated machines contain screws, too. They can also contain other types of simple machines.

Fastening screws and nuts and bolts hold together the parts of almost all complex machines. These fasteners are often put in place by robots on factory assembly lines. If you have a bicycle, try counting how many nuts, bolts, and screws hold it together.

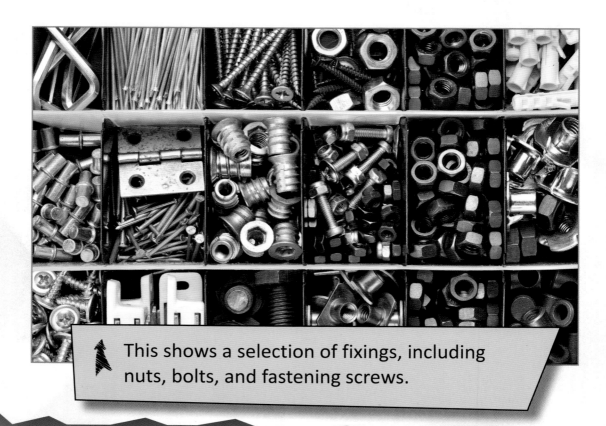

This shows a selection of fixings, including nuts, bolts, and fastening screws.

Adjusting with screws

Screw threads are often used to carefully adjust the position of certain parts of machines. For example, binoculars, telescopes, and microscopes are all focused using screw threads. When you turn a screw just a small amount, the screw thread moves by an even smaller amount. So, the thread can adjust the position of something very accurately.

Turning the focusing screw on a microscope moves the lenses very slowly up or down.

LEVELING WITH SCREWS

Many machines, such as ovens and washing machines, have feet that are fixed on screws. When a foot is turned, it raises or lowers that corner of the machine so that the machine can be made level.

FACTS AND FUN

AMAZING SCREWS

Some of the largest bolts ever made were 27 feet (8.3 meters) long, 4 feet (1.3 meters) in diameter, and weighed more than 13 tons. They were used to bolt two oil tankers together.

Mountaineers carry special ice screws that they screw into ice. They can tie their ropes to the end of the screw.

Huge augers are used to drill long underground tunnels more than 6½ feet (2 meters) wide for water pipes.

A combine harvester has a screw conveyor at the front. The conveyor gathers up chopped-down crops and feeds them into the machine.

One of the smallest screws ever made is just 1 millimeter long and a tenth of a millimeter across. In your hand, it would look like a speck of dust!

SCREWS TODAY

All simple machines, including screws, were invented thousands of years ago. The screw was invented about 2,000 years ago. At first, screws were used in devices to press olives to make olive oil and to press grapes for making wine. Screws are even more important today because they hold together complex machines and so many other things. There's no doubt that screws will be useful for many years to come.

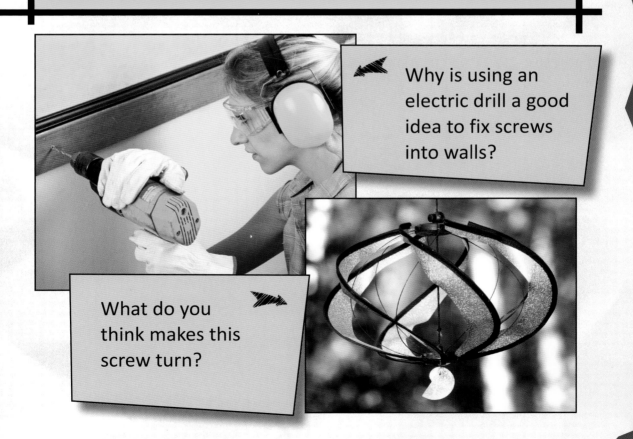

Why is using an electric drill a good idea to fix screws into walls?

What do you think makes this screw turn?

GLOSSARY

bolt rod with a screw thread and a head at one end

clockwise movement in the same direction as the hands of a clock

counterclockwise movement in the opposite direction of the hands of a clock

fastening screw type of screw used to fix objects to materials, or to attach two pieces of material together

lever long bar that is pushed or pulled against a fulcrum to help move heavy loads or cut material

nut disc of material with a hole in the center that has a screw thread on the inside and will fit onto a bolt

pulley simple machine made up of wheels and rope, used to lift or pull objects

ramp simple machine used to lift heavy objects

spring device that can be pressed or pulled but returns to its first shape when released

wedge simple machine used to split apart materials

wheel and axle simple machine made up of a wheel on a rod, used to turn or lift objects

FIND OUT MORE

Books

Deane-Pratt, Ade. *Simple Machines* (How Things Work).
New York: PowerKids, 2012.

Oxlade, Chris. *Screws* (Simple Machines). North
Mankato, Minn.: Smart Apple Media, 2008.

Walker, Sally M., and Roseann Feldmann. *Put Screws
to the Test* (How Do Simple Machines Work?).
Minneapolis: Lerner, 2012.

Web sites

Facthound offers a safe, fun way to find
Internet sites related to this book. All
of the sites on Facthound have been
researched by our staff.

Here's all you do:
Visit *www.facthound.com*
Type in this code: 9781410968166

INDEX